A souvenir guide

Blickling Estate

Norfolk

 **National Trust**

A Tour Through His...
3   The beginnings of B...
4   Early connections

Building Blickling   6
7   Tudor into Jacobean
8   Sir Henry Hobart, 1st Baronet
10 Sir Henry's house
12 Lavish interiors
14 The formal garden
15 Drawing on the estate

Embellishing Blickling   16
17 Sir Henry Hobart, 4th Baronet
18 John Hobart, 1st Earl of Buckinghamshire
20 Recovering fortunes
22 The 1st Earl's inheritance
23 Grand plans
24 Henrietta Howard
25 John Hobart, 2nd Earl of Buckinghamshire
26 Return from Russia
28 State rooms
30 Gardening on a grand scale
31 The wider estate

Conserving Blickling   34
35 Caroline, Lady Suffield
36 In remembrance
38 William, 8th Marquess of Lothian and Lady Constance Talbot
40 William's improvements
42 A long widowhood

Bequeathing Blickling   44
45 A visionary thinker
46 Philip Kerr, 11th Marquess of Lothian
48 The Marquess makes good
50 The Marquess in the garden
51 Norah Lindsay
52 An oral archive
54 The RAF at Oulton
55 The estate in wartime

Presenting Blickling   56
57 Vision and ambition
58 Keeping the garden trim and true
60 A view into the past
62 Managing the land
64 A complete picture

A Tour Through History

Nobody ever forgets their first sight of the mansion at Blickling. The famous gables and the embracing yew offer a welcome that softens the grandeur of a consciously fashionable façade. But the house, while the heart, is only part of an estate with a history stretching back over a thousand years.

The beginnings of Blickling

We've briefly introduced the main cast of characters who built and shaped and saved Blickling, creating this beautiful landscape that we can all enjoy today. But as well as being remarkable for the individuals who called Blickling home, the estate is fascinating for what it represents as a whole. The landscape, with its hedges and narrow tree-lined lanes, has changed little over the centuries and is quintessentially Norfolk. This does not make it a living museum, however, isolated from the modern world – it continues to act as a hub of social and economic activity, providing homes and work for local families.

In the beginning

The history of the estate, today covering over 2,000 hectares (almost 5,000 acres), stretches back to past millennia, and there is evidence of the everyday as well as recorded links to significant events in this country's history.

Archaeological finds, such as arrowheads, axe heads and pieces of Roman pottery and burnt flint, have provided evidence of human occupation from the Neolithic period (c.4000–2500BC). The site seems a sensible choice for early occupation: in Old English, Blickling can be interpreted to mean a grassy bank next to a stream, 'blick' being related to beck and 'ling' being the grassy bank.

Blickling from the beginning was home to people who would play key roles in history: in the 11th century it was the site of a manor house that belonged to Harold Godwinson (later to become King of England). Some time after Harold's defeat at the Battle of Hastings,

William I gave it to his chaplain. However, this would not be the only time that Blickling could claim a royal connection.

HARALDUS II
Regierte bey seines Vertriebnen Vatters Leb Zeiten und Verrichte-te nichts Löbliches.

Opposite The entrance front of Blickling and its 400-year-old yew

Above Harold Godwinson, later King Harold II, had his home at Blickling

Early connections

By 1091 King Harold's manor house had become the summer palace of the bishops of Norwich. Towards the end of the 14th century, Sir Nicholas Dagworth (an important aide to Edward III) settled at Blickling, and had a rectangular, moated house built. It must have been a rather grand house, owned as it was by several well-connected individuals.

By the beginning of the 15th century Blickling was the property of Sir John Fastolfe (1380–1459). Sir John was an English knight during the Hundred Years War and one of the most powerful men in Norfolk. However, he has enjoyed a more lasting reputation as the inspiration for Shakespeare's comic character Falstaff, who appears in three plays (the two Henry IV plays and *The Merry Wives of Windsor*). In each the character is a fat, vain, boastful and cowardly knight, who spends most of his time drinking, living on stolen or borrowed money.

Whether the fictional character resembled Sir John in these respects is not known, but the later owners of Blickling, the Hobarts, were apparently pleased with the connection to the original Fastolfe, and in later remodellings introduced references to his ownership: his crest and arms appear in the Brown Drawing Room chimneypiece, the early 15th-century carving originally from Sir John's Caister Castle in Great Yarmouth. What is known with certainty is that Sir John sold Blickling in 1452 to Geoffrey Boleyn, the bearer of another very famous name.

Monumental events

In 1505 Blickling was inherited by Geoffrey's grandson Sir Thomas Boleyn, whose daughter Anne became the second wife of Henry VIII in 1533, with enormous consequence to the country's history.

Since Anne's date of birth has never been confirmed it is not certain where she was born, whether here at Blickling or at Hever Castle, in Kent. Regardless, the Hobarts claimed Blickling as her birthplace and again created monuments celebrating this connection.

As the events that resulted from Henry VIII's divorce from his first wife and the Catholic Church so completely affected every aspect of life in England, including the public imagination, what is true and what is fabricated can be difficult to tell apart. For example, the late 18th-century mahogany pole-screen in the O Room contains a piece of ancient black velvet worked with the legend: 'A piece of the bed in which Anne Boleyn was born at Blickling 15… Beheaded 19th May 1536.' The fabric in fact dates from the 1560s.

Above Sir John Fastolfe's coat of arms in the Brown Drawing Room; later owners celebrated Sir John's connection with Blickling

Swift change of fortune

Because of the ardent interest King Henry had in Sir Thomas' daughter, great honours were bestowed upon him: first Treasurer of the Household, then Knight of the Garter, Viscount Rochford and finally, in 1529, the earldom of Wiltshire. The future looked promising for the Boleyns, but just three years after the marriage, Anne was out of favour and it was off with her head. Sir Thomas died in 1539 and the property passed to relatives, the Cleres, also with failing fortunes. Sir Edward Clere died a bankrupt in 1605 and 11 years later his widow sold Blickling to Sir Henry Hobart.

As mentioned above, some connections are real, some are fancied, but still it is tempting to make the link between the events that saw a young woman of Blickling catching the eye of a king, her family reaping great benefits, and the boost to Blickling's fortunes resulting from a royal liaison two centuries later.

Left Seen in the Great Hall, the carved figure of Anne Boleyn on a plinth inscribed *Anna Boleyn Hic Nata*, 'Anne Boleyn was born here'

Below left Anne's father, Sir Thomas Boleyn

SꞬ Thoꞩ Bullen Earl of Wiltshire & Ormond

Headless hosts

Anne Boleyn is said to haunt her ancestral home on the anniversary of her execution. As the clock strikes midnight she appears in a coach driven by a headless coachman and four headless horses. Anne is of course similarly headless. Her father, Sir Thomas, is also said to haunt hereabouts, having been cursed for taking no action to prevent two of his children being executed by Henry VIII. Each year his ghost has to attempt to cross 12 bridges before cockcrow. His frantic route takes him from Blickling to Aylsham, Burgh, Buxton, Coltishall, Meyton, Oxnead and Wroxham.

Building Blickling

By the end of the Elizabethan period, Blickling was already picked out as a scene of significant events. A wealthy and well-connected lawyer had had his eye on it for some time and had a vision to create something fit for the family name for generations to come.

Tudor into Jacobean

Opposite **Blickling attained Sir Henry's far-reaching vision although he was never able to see it for himself**

Below **Sir Nicholas Dagworth**

Sir Nicholas Dagworth's house was built in the 14th century but its plan and structure can still be seen in the mansion house that came some 300 years after. When Blickling was sold to Sir Henry Hobart in 1616, he might have been expected to level the house that came with the estate to make way for a new house that matched his ambition. It certainly would have made the job easier for his architect, Robert Lyminge, and perhaps less costly. But it seems part of Sir Henry's vision for the house was something that retained and celebrated some of its history and august connections.

Lofty ambitions

Sir Henry's precise year of birth is not known, but it's thought it was around 1560, so he was already quite elderly when he began the ambitious programme of creating a home to suit his status and to bear the Hobart family name. His London residence in Smithfield was rented from the Earl of Westmorland; he also lived some of the time in a house in Highgate, the freehold of which he was negotiating at the time of his death; in Norwich he held the lease for Chapelfield House. So he had waited quite some time before buying a property outright, perhaps suggesting his resolve to purchase Blickling.

He certainly wasted no time putting his mark on the place, quite literally with the initials H for Henry and D for his wife Dorothy, I for his son John and P for his daughter-in-law Philippa on the south, or entrance, front. The dates 1619 and 1620 – the years the walls went up and the roof went on – are prominently placed too, Sir Henry establishing himself as the founder of an estate with a dynastic future. Sadly, he did not see the finished work, visiting the house only once in August 1624 (he died in March 1626), but his vision was one his descendants would embrace and carry on.

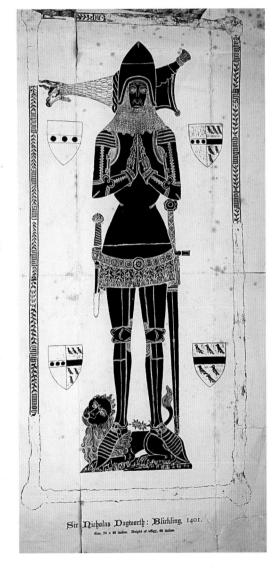

Sir Nicholas Dagworth: Blickling, 1401.
Size, 75 × 25 inches. Height of effigy, 66 inches.

Sir Henry Hobart, 1st Baronet (d.1626)

Above Sir Henry Hobart, 1st Baronet by Daniel Mytens

The origin of the name Hobart (pronounced Hubbard) is old German and means 'mind bright'. Early Hobarts certainly demonstrated strong ambition and mental keenness, and Sir Henry Hobart came from a long line of distinguished lawyers. His own successful and lucrative career meant he could set about establishing a family seat. The little statues of Justice, with a sword and scales, and Prudence, with a mirror, that he included on the entrance front of the house he built suggest that it was intended to celebrate his achievements. The other insignia that go with the Hobart name are the bulls, the family crest, scattered about the property; the bulls on the bridge over the moat before the entrance (see opposite) proudly announce this is the home of the Hobarts. Coincidentally, an alternative spelling of Boleyn – the famous family who once lived at Blickling – was Bullen, and they too had bulls as part of their coat of arms.

Sir Henry became Lord Chief Justice of the Common Pleas in 1611 and was granted the hereditary title of baronet in the same year by James I – one of the very first to be created, as the king was fundraising for military campaigns in Ireland at the time. Sir Henry bought the Blickling estate in 1616, but he must have been aware of it for some time; in 1590 he married Dorothy Bell in Blickling church, even though her parish was some distance away in Upwell, in the far west of the county, and his own family seat was south of Norwich. He bought some land in the Blickling parish in 1606 but he only got his hands on the hall a decade later, quickly setting about an ambitious programme of remodelling.

The Hobart bulls on the moat at the hall's entrance

Sir Henry's house

Sir Henry bought the estate for £5,500 and proceeded to spend almost twice that amount on remodelling the house. But despite Sir Henry's vision for a house and estate that would bear the family name for generations to come, he sought to incorporate the old in the new.

In the 1620s architect Robert Lyminge was employed to re-design the house, receiving a daily wage of 2s 6d. As already mentioned, part of the brief was to incorporate much of the existing medieval fabric into the new Jacobean building. This was unusual although not unprecedented. Sir Henry's decision to keep the moat rather than elevating the site to create the far-reaching views favoured by many builders of the period shows perhaps a degree of attachment to the old house and its history.

This presented Lyminge with a real challenge; however Sir Henry had gone to one of the country's most experienced architects. The narrow entrance front, behind which was an awkwardly small courtyard, and a staircase that gave access to the upper floor in an inconvenient place for the design of a main reception area – all these were tackled and incorporated in the magnificent red-brick house with leaded-light windows, many turrets and extravagant gables, that gradually developed.

Above Sir Henry's east front designed by Robert Lyminge

Lavish expenditure

Accounts show that Sir Henry lavished a fortune on materials and the finest craftsmanship to work them to best effect. He started with the south and east fronts, rebuilding them between 1619 and 1626 in red brick and limestone from Ketton in Rutland. This creamy yellow limestone had been particularly favoured by the architects of the Cambridge colleges. Paving stone came from even further afield, from Purbeck in Dorset; lead came from Derbyshire, iron from Sussex and glass from Newcastle.

Building work started at a pace and so did the costs of assembling all these materials. In the first two years Sir Henry spent over £4,000, almost as much as he paid for the entire estate. The building of the house itself cost just short of £8,000.

The projecting wings, not begun until 1624, came at a cost of just under £1,000 apiece. Considering these were service wings, it might seem surprising that so much was lavished on them, their façades no less embellished than those of the main house. That they were added well after the building of the main house had started suggests they were a development not in the original plan. Likewise, their matching façades might have been the architect's solution to a problem posed by working within an existing structure (see over).

An evolving design

Elsewhere too it seems Lyminge had the freedom to deviate from plan, if it enhanced the overall design. A note dated 29 November 1619 records changes to the original specification, including Lyminge's appeal not to have a brick wall with battlements in front of the moat and the entrance front. Lyminge worried this would look 'very lumpish and will take away the prospect of the lower part of the house' and argued for an 'open work of stone'. He got his wish but sadly the wall does not survive; the matching pierced stonework of the entrance bridge is all there is to show how it would have looked.

Above Hatfield House, another of Lyminge's designs

Below The open, pierced stonework of the bridge that was Lyminge's suggested alternative to Sir Henry's battlements

Lavish interiors

As the exterior of Blickling and the entrance front in particular have the power to halt first-time visitors in their tracks, we can suppose that the interior of Sir Henry's house was equally ostentatious. Certainly he had no shortage of money to realise his vision, but it's an interior we have to imagine, as later remodellings removed nearly all trace of it.

In terms of the arrangement of rooms, we know that Lyminge followed the conventions found in Elizabethan and Jacobean houses, but he cleverly deviated in certain places to get around the awkwardness of incorporating parts of the Tudor house.

Although Blickling might look generously proportioned to most who first encounter it, the entrance front is rather narrow. As well as the tight little Tudor courtyard Lyminge had the further issue of a staircase positioned in such a way that it was impossible to arrange the principal rooms on the first floor of the house as a continuous suite.

His solution was to have the Long Gallery in the east range with the best view of the garden, and the great chamber, withdrawing chamber and principal bedchamber on the entrance front. This less-than-ideal arrangement may have been the reason for the aforementioned service ranges. These ranges, each 69m (225ft) long, created a grand forecourt and gave the occupants of these private rooms in the main house some distance from the outside world.

Left The Long Gallery

Worthily decorated

On into the retained Tudor courtyard (or Stone Court as it came to be called in the 17th century to distinguish it from a rear courtyard), and thence into the Great Hall, the principal room of a Jacobean house. There was no staircase here at that time, Lyminge having situated it in an ante-room off what was a generously sized parlour (now the Dining Room), another important room with a massive fireplace bearing Sir Henry's arms and motto.

Naturally the house was decorated with great ostentation, although only fragments survive, recycled and repurposed by later occupants. We know of plaster figures of the Nine Worthies, warriors and leaders epitomising virtue and valour, descriptions of which were included in a letter by John Hobart, 2nd Earl of Buckinghamshire (see page 25) when he remodelled the Great Hall: 'Some tributory sorrow should be paid to the nine worthies; but Hector has lost his spear and his nose, David his harp, Godfrey of Boulogne his ears, Alexander the Great his highest shoulder, and part of Joshua's belly is fallen in. As the ceiling is to be raised eight of them must have gone, and Hector is at all events determined to leave his niche.'

The Long Gallery

This was the showroom of the house, the most lavishly appointed and elaborately decorated with the best views of the garden. Stretching 37m (123ft) in length, the Long Gallery may appear to the modern visitor a spacious corridor, but it was designed as a room to be used in its own right, for entertaining guests, for taking exercise when the weather was bad, and for displaying art collections. Its original fireplace was removed in the mid-18th century, and even that replacement was taken out. However, the main attraction still stands, or rather floats above head-height. Edward Stanyon was contracted to produce four ceilings at Blickling for the most prestigious rooms: the Long Gallery, Sir Henry's great chamber (now the South Drawing Room), the parlour (now the Dining Room but with the loss of its original ceiling) and Sir Henry's withdrawing chamber next to his bedroom (later remodelled, again the ceiling lost).

The ceiling in the Long Gallery cost Sir Henry £95 19s (the Hobart bull in the turret closet off the Long Gallery was done at a lower rate of 4s 6d). Sir Henry's coat of arms and motto occur in alternate panels down the centre of the ceiling and within intricately patterned bands are panels depicting morally improving scenes from *Minerva Britanna, Or A Garden Of Heroical Deuises, furnished, and adorned with Emblemes and Impresa's of sundry natures* (1612). From over 200 verses and accompanying emblems Sir Henry chose, among others, for his ceiling: womanly beauty and the power of love, kingly majesty and kingly cares, divine wisdom and pity, the need to trust God and to avoid hypocrites.

The formal garden

Since the 17th century the main garden has been to the east of the house, affording the Long Gallery, the summit of Sir Henry's decorative ambition, the best views within and without.

It seems Sir Henry had plans for the design of his garden, just as he had a vision for his house. After he acquired the estate in 1616, he remodelled the gardens to include ponds, wilderness and a parterre.

A large square of water once lay before the north front and was known as the 'Wilderness Pond', a clue as to what bordered the banks of this man-made water feature. This was later filled in but is visible on a survey commissioned a century later (see page 23).

Taking Blickling's flat landscape into account, Sir Henry also had a garden mount created – an artificial hill to provide views of the new garden. This was largely demolished in 1688–9, but its remains may be indicated by a curve at the northern end of the Parterre.

A garden to impress

A surviving drawing for a 'banketting house' by Lyminge (see right) suggests that Sir Henry wanted to use the garden to impress and entertain his visitors, and intended to leave his mark on the landscape surrounding his house.

The same drawing indicates a walk from this feature to a 'wilderness'. The concept of a wilderness is much more structured than its name implies, and would not have been a tangle of shrubs and trees but a geometric layout of walks and hedges.

Other clues about Sir Henry's vanished garden include a sum of money paid in 1620 to one Thomas Larger for a white marble fountain which, given the amount, was likely to have been on a grand scale.

Drawing on the estate

The estate that Sir Henry bought with Sir Nicholas' house was probably about 100 acres (40 hectares) in size but he had plans for the extension of the estate just as he had for the house. However, the land was initially put to good use providing for the building of Blickling Hall.

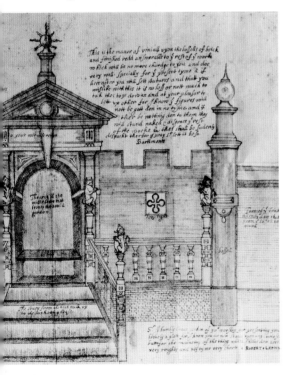

Although the materials used to dress the house came from all over the country, the essential building materials were provided by the estate. Then, as is often the case now, sourcing locally made good economic sense.

Three brick kilns were specially constructed on the estate. In 1619 when building started, 823,000 bricks were produced at a cost of 5s per thousand; the following year 465,000 were fired and in 1621–2, as the house was nearing completion, 125,000 more. It's estimated that the service wings that followed a couple of years later required a million more bricks.

Other than brick, timber was the basic construction material used for the house. A survey was carried out of 'ye parke & wood & other grounds' and by early May 1619, 308 trees had been felled. However, more wood was required and the following year timber was being sourced from Morley, presumed to be Swanton Morley 17 miles away, and Langley, the estate of a Hobart relative.

Sir Henry set out his vision for a grand estate in support of the family home, but as he didn't live to see even the house built, it was left to his descendants to pursue his ambition. By the time the estate came to the National Trust it would extend to 2,000 hectares (almost 5,000 acres).

Opposite The Parterre viewed from the Wilderness, dating from the earliest Jacobean garden

Below left Robert Lyminge's only surviving design for Blickling, dated 1623, for a 'banketting house', or covered garden seat, which no longer survives

Embellishing Blickling

Sir Henry, 1st Baronet, built Blickling to suit his station and also to provide a fitting family seat for generations of Hobarts to come. With one notable exception, the Hobarts continued to win favour in high circles, improving their fortunes and using Blickling to display their wealth and status.

Below *Peter the Great triumphing over the defeated Swedish army at Poltawa in 1709* – a gift to John Hobart, 2nd Earl of Buckinghamshire, displayed in a specially designed state room

Sir Henry Hobart, 4th Baronet (d.1698)

Above Sir Henry Hobart, 4th Baronet; attributed to William Wissing

Sir Henry Hobart, 4th Baronet, was the great-grandson of Sir Henry, 1st Baronet. This Henry had the honour of being knighted by Charles II soon after the Restoration in 1671. He was a politician and a member of the Whig party, and entered the House of Commons for King's Lynn in 1681, sitting for it until 1685.

He inherited Blickling and the baronetcy from his father in 1683, when the estate was deeply in debt. By 1683 the estate at Blickling was only a quarter of the size it had been in 1625 due to debts, but a dowry of £10,000, gained through marriage, temporarily solved the problem. In 1684 he married Elizabeth Maynard, eldest daughter of prominent politician Sir Joseph Maynard. It was a good marriage and helped him pay off the mortgage, make some alterations to the house and carry out significant landscaping of the park. They had eight children, four of which survived. The eldest was Henrietta, who would far exceed her father's ability to impress or influence (see page 24).

Indeed, Sir Henry had a reputation for being rather quarrelsome. When he lost his county seat at the election of 1698, he placed the blame on rumours about his conduct at the Battle of the Boyne. Sir Henry accused his neighbour Oliver Le Neve, a lawyer from Great Witchingham who was known as a great sportsman and a great drinker, of spreading these rumours, and challenged him to a duel. This illegal contest (due to the absence of any seconds or witnesses) was the last of its kind in Norfolk and took place on Cawston Heath on 20 August 1698. Le Neve fought left-handed and was soon wounded in the arm by Sir Henry, who had a reputation as a swordsman. However, Le Neve then struck back and ran Sir Henry through. Sir Henry was carried home to Blickling where he died of his injuries the following day. His opponent was found guilty of manslaughter. Le Neve fled to Holland, but was later pardoned and returned to England two years later.

It is said that details of the duel came from a girl who was hiding in the bushes. The event is commemorated by the Duel Stone, inscribed 'HH', which stands in a small National Trust-owned plot near the Woodrow Garage in Cawston.

John Hobart,
1st Earl of Buckinghamshire
(1693–1756)

When John was just five years old, his father was killed in a duel (see previous page) and John inherited his father's title. The estate was put in trust until he came of age, and the steward, John Brewster, seems to have done a good job of not only caretaking but also, under his more careful management, helping the finances of the estate recover. Some important heirlooms had been sold, but in 1703 a total of 13 pictures were bought back, including the portrait of the builder of Blickling, Sir Henry, by Daniel Mytens (see page 8).

After completing his education at Cambridge in 1713, Sir John spent a year travelling Europe. In 1717 he settled down and took a wife, Judith Britiffe. Judith died when their son, also John, was only four and Sir John remarried. With Elizabeth Bristow he had a son, George, who would inherit the title of earl but not Blickling.

Sir John followed in his father's political footsteps and became a Member of Parliament for St Ives from 1715–27 and for Norfolk from 1727–8. In 1746 he was made Earl of Buckinghamshire, allegedly helped by the fact that his sister, Henrietta Howard, was the long-term mistress of King George II (see page 24).

He celebrated his status by commissioning William Aikman to paint full-length portraits of his sister and many Norfolk dignitaries, such as Thomas Coke, Earl of Leicester and Sir Robert Walpole. These portraits were first displayed in the Long Gallery, the natural and most prominent place for displaying such treasures. When Sir John later inherited over 10,000 books from his distant cousin, Sir Richard Ellys of Nocton, the Long Gallery was the only room in the hall large enough to display this vast collection, so he removed the portraits to other areas of the house. For more on Blickling's library (see page 22).

Left John, 1st Earl of
Buckinghamshire; by John
Theodore Heins Senior

Recovering fortunes

Although the quarrelsome baronet, Sir Henry, inherited his father's debts and Blickling was mortgaged to a London merchant, his marriage temporarily rescued the situation. Further boosts to Blickling's fortunes came by virtue of women of wealth and influence.

Sir Henry appears to have run the house and estate with a community of local people in his employ: In the house Widow Kytchen was tasked with 'looking to the Rooms and Furniture'; in the garden, William Trappit oversaw women and children weeding the beds; while on the estate John Canseller was given the job of rat-catcher.

Sir Henry did little to the house but paid a glazier, Thomas Knowles, to maintain its many windows, and employed Thomas Burrows the carpenter, who was kept busy on the estate felling trees and building farmhouses and bridges. There were some necessary repairs in 1695 when the front door, which had been positioned in the left-hand turret, had to be relocated to its central position when that turret began to suffer subsidence.

Extensive planting

Sir Henry seems to have expended some money and energy on the gardens and park too. In the 1680s there appears to have been a momentary surplus of cash – perhaps from the dowry of his marriage in 1684 – and there was extensive planting in the park. The Wilderness, as well as the grand avenues of trees seen on James Corbridge's 1729 survey (see page 23), are thought to date to this time. A great storm of the 1680s which uprooted many trees may have contributed to this replanting.

Records also show large sums of money being spent on items for the garden such as new balustrading, 'My Ladies new Garden Next the Dovehouse' – a wedding present bought with her family's money perhaps – and pots for orange trees.

Continuing fortune

Sir Henry's marriage might have helped rescue Blickling; his untimely death might also have saved the estate from mismanagement. Shortly after Sir John came into his inheritance, which had had a careful custodian in steward John Brewster, Blickling received another boost from another good marriage. Judith Britiffe was daughter of the Recorder of Norwich and came with a large dowry of £15,000.

Further good fortune came when Sir John's sister (see page 24) found favour at the court of George I. Henrietta was witty and attractive but unhappily married. She became the mistress of the king's son, the Prince of Wales, and this had happy consequences for her younger brother, who was made a Knight of the Bath in 1725, Treasurer of the Chamber in 1727 and Baron Hobart of Blickling in 1728.

Now Lord Hobart had the means to announce his exalted position in society through the acquisition of fine furnishings and commissioning of portraits from the best artists of the day.

Clockwise from above Henry Kelsall (1692–1762); Sir Thomas Saunders Sebright (1692–1736), 4th Bt; Sir William Leman (d.1741), 2nd Bt of Northaw; Thomas Coke (1697–1759), 1st Earl of Leicester; Sir John Cope (1690–1760); Field Marshal Sir Robert Rich (1685–1768), 4th Bt; Sir Robert Walpole (1676–1745), 1st Earl of Orford; Colonel Harbord Harbord (1675?–1742): some of the portraits of Sir John's illustrious friends by William Aikman

Portraits of prosperity

Henrietta's portrait in masquerade dress (see page 24) attributed to Thomas Gibson is one of a series of portraits of Hobart's friends, relatives and political allies. Others were painted by William Aikman, the son and heir of a Scottish laird who sold his estates to become a painter, and indeed made quite a name for himself. The frames either by or at least in the style of William Kent, the leading architect and designer of early Georgian Britain, and the original positioning of the portraits in the Long Gallery, all were intended to impress.

The 1st Earl's inheritance

The Long Gallery, created by Sir Henry, was always the best room in the house, so when Sir John inherited a library that was one of the greatest collections of its kind, this room was the obvious repository.

The inheritance came in about 1745 from a distant cousin, Sir Richard Ellys, and Sir John decided to convert the Long Gallery to a library, sparing no expense in the process.

A group of craftsmen was employed and Joseph Pickford made an expensive marble fireplace; Peter Scheemakers, whose notable work includes William Shakespeare's memorial in Westminster Abbey, created a bust of Sir Richard Ellys; Francis Hayman, one of the founding members of the Royal Academy in 1768, provided a series of paintings over the doors; and the sculptor John Cheere produced a total of 28 busts, 20 vases and three statues.

Blickling's library

The collection is enormous, with approximately 12,500 volumes, but perhaps the library's most prized possession is a copy of Suetonius' *The Twelve Caesars*, essentially a piece of historical gossip from the first century AD. Handwritten on vellum (or animal skin to lesser bibliophiles), the book was produced in 1450 for Borso D'Este, the Duke of Ferrara and one of the great men of the Italian Renaissance. Featuring exquisite gold-leaf decoration and painted pictures (see left), the manuscript was a medieval showpiece.

The oldest book in the library is a handwritten manuscript from the 1100s containing the Dialogues of Pope Gregory the Great. It is most notable for a short paragraph containing the Apostles' Creed in a mix of Old English (Anglo-Saxon) and early Middle English, one of the earliest known versions. This was written at a time when English was being superseded by French as the official language under the rule of the Norman conquerors.

Grand plans

The 1st Earl was too busy scaling Georgian society to make much of an impact on the house – his only significant addition was the library. However, in the early 18th century the garden was quite transformed.

By the time the 1st Earl came into his inheritance, the estate ran to 160 acres (65 hectares). He set about expanding the park and adding features. The lake, first mentioned in 1711 when he was 18 years old, may have been one of his first projects. That he had a master plan for the park might be inferred from the detailed survey that the Earl had drawn up in 1729 by James Corbridge.

This shows the landscape significantly altered since Sir Henry's time. His house and garden were arranged on a north–south axis, but in Corbridge's survey the whole garden has been turned through 180 degrees. The old square Wilderness Pond remained but now a grand avenue of trees ran from the house to a Doric temple. The temple is first mentioned by a visitor in 1738 but was probably built some ten years before. Clearly visible from the 1st Earl's new library, it was presumably his addition. In 1730–35, William Kent was designing the house and garden buildings at nearby Holkham Hall for Thomas Coke, 1st Earl of Leicester, and the temples at Holkham and Blickling are identical in their proportions and details. However, the architect, whether Kent or Matthew Brettingham who worked with him, added details personal to his client, so in the frieze is the Earl's monogram alternating with the Hobart bull.

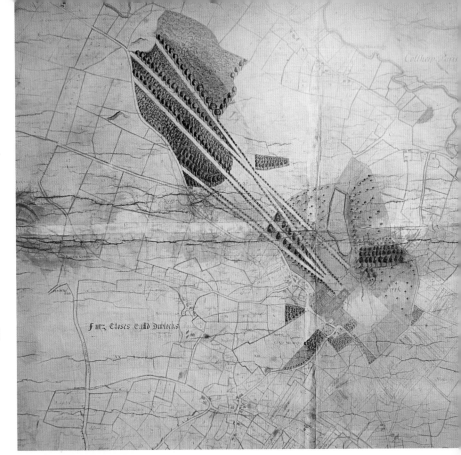

Furz Closes called Dublocks

Opposite Sir Richard Ellys, the benefactor of Blickling's library

Above James Corbridge's 1729 survey showing an avenue of trees and a 'New Pond'

Left The Doric Temple

Henrietta Howard (1688–1767)

Above Henrietta Howard, Countess of Suffolk; attributed to Thomas Gibson, c.1720

Henrietta's mother died in 1701, three years after the 4th Baronet's duel to the death, leaving her the oldest of four orphans. In 1706, in a bid to improve her family's fortunes, she was married to Charles Howard, the youngest son of the Earl of Suffolk. They had one son, Henry Howard, 10th Earl of Suffolk, but the marriage was an unhappy one, as Charles was said to be a wife-beater and compulsive gambler.

In 1714 Henrietta and her husband gained a position in the Royal Household of the Prince of Wales at St James' Palace. Their marriage continued to deteriorate, and Henrietta left Charles in 1717, at which time she was banned from seeing her son Henry.

Between about 1718 and 1734, Henrietta was the mistress of the Prince of Wales (from 1727, George II). She became the centre of a wide circle of noble and literary friends including Alexander Pope, John Gay and Jonathan Swift, and was described by Horace Walpole as 'of a just height, well made, extremely fair, with the finest light brown hair'.

In 1731, Henrietta became Countess of Suffolk. She left royal service in 1734 and married George Berkeley a year later, a happy but short marriage since he died in 1746. Henrietta continued to live in Twickenham, at Marble Hill, a villa given to her by the Prince of Wales. Her brother's son, John, spent much time with her here, perhaps a comfort given that she had been prevented from seeing her own son. She lived there until her death, but given her closeness to her nephew was very much involved in remodelling Blickling in 1765.

John Hobart, 2nd Earl of Buckinghamshire (1723–93)

Above John, 2nd Earl of Buckinghamshire, in his robes as Lord Lieutenant of Ireland; by Thomas Gainsborough, 1784

Much of John Hobart's early life was spent at his aunt Henrietta's home at Marble Hill, his mother having died when he was four. Henrietta had a great influence on him, cultivating his interest in the arts in all their forms.

John inherited the Blickling estate at the age of 33. He had no financial worries, his father, the 1st Earl, having left the estate in good economic order. His early life saw him involved in international politics, though some questioned his abilities. Walpole, who was so complimentary about his aunt, referred to him as 'fat, fair, sweet, and seen through in an instant'. In his forties, he made the arduous journey to the court of Catherine the Great of Russia, serving as George II's ambassador there.

On his return to Blickling, he made extensive changes to the house, introducing the classical aesthetic of his day, also much favoured by his aunt, whilst respecting its Jacobean character. In the new rooms he created are mementos of his time in Russia.

He married firstly Mary Anne Drury, daughter of Sir Thomas Drury, 1st Baronet, and secondly Caroline, daughter of William James Conolly, but died without surviving sons and the title of earl went to his half-brother George. However Blickling passed to his daughter Caroline (see page 35), having passed over her older sister, Harriet. Caroline was perhaps the more attentive daughter and certainly she honoured his memory, building a family mausoleum (see page 36), in which her father and his two wives were laid to rest.

Return from Russia

On his return to Blickling, the 2nd Earl made extensive changes to the house, whilst respecting the house's Jacobean character. He engaged Thomas Ivory and his son William, and correspondence with his aunt shows she had quite a hand in the remodelling.

The time John spent with Henrietta did much to inform his tastes. Marble Hill was a highly fashionable Palladian villa, that style strongly influenced by the classical aesthetic with a particular focus on symmetry. So when John thought to remodel his house, some of this character was brought to Blickling.

He regularly consulted with his aunt about the renovations and clearly valued her opinions. In one letter he wrote: 'Lady Buckinghamshire [his first wife] and Lady Dorothy [his sister] have entered into a conspiracy against the old chimney piece in the eating-room. Their little intrigues can never shake my settled purpose, but they tease me and your authority is necessary to silence them.'

Above The south front of Marble Hill House, Twickenham

Left The Great Hall remodelled with a double-flight staircase in 1767; watercolour by John Chessel Buckler, 1829

Social success

John came into his inheritance at the age of 33, but at that time was pursuing a career in international politics. In August 1762 he was posted to St Petersburg as Ambassador at the court of Catherine the Great. He seems to have had some of his aunt's social graces and socially he was a success. His duties left him plenty of time to enjoy balls and other social occasions, garnering popularity at the highest levels, and he came away from his service with various gifts that would be proudly displayed at Blickling.

An eye to history

When John returned to Blickling in the autumn of 1764, he set about a programme of repairs and modernisations. William Ivory's design, drawn up in 1765, for a remodelled north front shows a symmetrical arrangement of windows and pediments from the classical aesthetic, but the Jacobean turrets remained an important feature.

Internally, the single biggest change was the relocation of the staircase to the Great Hall. In 1767 it was rebuilt as a grand double flight, incorporating nearly all the timbers of the old Jacobean staircase, demonstrating John's desire to retain that aspect of the house's historical character. Some of the figures on the newel posts are from the Jacobean staircase, but others are in a distinctly more modern style. To accommodate this grand staircase and help visitors more fully appreciate it, the front wall of the Great Hall was moved out into the Stone Court. But for all the modernisations, John kept the history of the house in mind, and it was this antiquarian view that inspired the two reliefs of Queen Elizabeth and her mother Anne Boleyn, set in niches in the wall of the Great Hall facing the entrance.

Above A newel post figure of a man in chain mail with pike and shield, c.1767

Above William Ivory's 1765 design for the north front of Blickling

Concessions to comfort

The 2nd Earl's remodelling of the house was intended to make it more impressive than ever, but there is evidence that people lived and relaxed here too. When the Jacobean staircase was removed, a comfortable suite of rooms was created on the ground floor of the east range. There was a 'Drinking Room' (the present Lower Ante-Room), next to which Lady Buckinghamshire had her dressing room and bedchamber (the present Brown Room). His Lordship evidently enjoyed carpentry and he had his 'Tool Closet' where he could enjoy his hobby. Somewhat bizarrely, further along the corridor was the 'Physic closet', containing a device 'for Electrifying'; the receiving of mild electric shocks was a health fad in the late 18th century. After a stimulating session here, the Earl could retire to his study, connected to his library in the Long Gallery above by a staircase installed in the corner turret in 1773.

State rooms

While the 2nd Earl's antiquarian touches demonstrate a regard for his house's history, he was very pleased with his present achievements and used the house to proudly display the gifts awarded to him during his embassy to Russia.

John's remodelling of the house was carried out over a number of years: he started in 1765, although he'd been consulting with architects for quite some time beforehand. He was made a widower and remarried in the interim. The first Lady Buckinghamshire died in 1769 (an inscription on the remodelled west front records that the bequest of her jewels paid for its completion) and John remarried the following year.

It wasn't until 1782 that he began finalising the decoration and furnishing of his finest room. If the Long Gallery was Sir Henry's showroom, then the Peter the Great Room was undoubtedly John's.

Prized possessions

In November 1778, another Ivory, the marble mason John, was commissioned to create 'a statuary sienna fireplace' to grace what was being referred to as the 'great room'. Adjoining the Long Gallery, the room that went on to become the Peter the Great Room occupies the three central bays of the first floor. Just as Sir Henry displayed his finest works of art in the Long Gallery, the 2nd Earl used this room to showcase his most prized possessions.

The spectacular tapestry, both in quality and scale, of *Peter the Great triumphing over the defeated Swedish army at Poltawa in 1709* (see page 16) was woven in St Petersburg in 1764, and given to John on the completion of his embassy. The portraits either side of the fireplace are by Thomas Gainsborough and depict the Earl and his second wife, Caroline Conolly.

For a room so clearly a celebration of a man's career, it may seem a less-than-masculine colour scheme, but the room was recorded in 1806 as 'having the four corner compartments with that in the middle… stained a delicate pink', presumably the fashion of the day. The carpet, an Axminster, seemingly followed the same fashion; given its proportions, it can only have been intended for this room.

Inner sanctum

Adjoining the Peter the Great Room is the State Bedroom. Occupying pride of place is the bed with tester and headboard made of a canopy of state given to John for his embassy to St Petersburg in 1763. Its positioning behind Ionic pillars creates an inner sanctum, emphasising the importance of its intended occupant. Neo-classical designs abound in this room, elevating its status and setting it apart from others. Another Axminster carpet, again made specifically for this room, features a border motif inspired by Roman murals.

A surfeit of riches

After completing his grandest suite of rooms, John spent the last decade of his life making small alterations and improvements to the house, introducing water closets in the early 1790s. He appears to have led a quiet life at Blickling, making good marriages for his four daughters.

The 2nd Earl's time in court had been largely spent socialising at balls and gatherings of wealthy nobility consuming equally rich food. It's possible his lifestyle caught up with him, as it is thought he died of gout, historically known as 'the disease of kings' or 'the rich man's disease'. According to Horace Walpole, the same man who described him as 'fat, fair, sweet', he died of a heart attack caused by thrusting an inflamed foot into a bucket of icy water.

Below The State Bedroom

Gardening on a grand scale

Above The Orangery, probably built by Samuel Wyatt in 1782

In 1765, the 2nd Earl gave the first Lady Buckinghamshire a flower garden to enjoy, full of 'Minionet Roses, mirtles and honeysuckles'. His plans for rest the of the garden and park were far more ambitious.

The 2nd Earl's most significant feature in the garden was the Orangery, built in 1782 to a design by Samuel Wyatt. Wyatt took over from Thomas and William Ivory when Thomas's leg was crushed by a piece of timber and his son William was called away to a colonial war with France. Wyatt was one of the leading exponents of Neo-classical design and it's possible that he had already been involved with Blickling's interiors; the State Bedroom (see previous page) is so markedly different from other rooms and especially confident in that style it suggests Wyatt's work.

The 1st Earl looked to Holkham Hall when he commissioned his own eyecatcher, a Doric temple, for the garden. Similarly, when the 2nd Earl was looking for inspiration, he found it at Holkham. Wyatt had designed a vine house there and Blickling's Orangery has borrowed features, such as the fanlights above the doors.

In the 1760s the 2nd Earl planted extensively in the park, blurring the previously geometric layout into something more naturalistic, with meandering paths and eye-catching features or seats and shelters. He also had the lake extended, in 1762, and it's thought that the spoil from the excavation was used to create the Mount on the east bank. Rising to a height of 10.5m (34ft) it afforded fine views. This feature may simply have been an obvious addition to a flat landscape, but it's tempting to think the 2nd Earl was following his forebear's vision of the park, replacing Sir Henry's viewing platform demolished in the 1680s (see page 14).

The wider estate

The 2nd Earl's extensive plans for the estate included the establishment of a deer park. Long popular among the English aristocracy, deer parks were almost an essential feature of any large country estate, a major status symbol as the landowner required a royal licence to create one.

The Earl's deer park extended westwards from the West Garden to Hyde Park and northwards towards Moorgate. As Blickling had ample land for more profitable agricultural use, the Hobarts could afford to set some aside for the 'emparkment' of deer.

The deer park no longer exists but part of it, Tower Park, gets its name from another recreational use intended to impress. As the Earl moved and entertained in the highest circles and had a large and largely flat park, it was fitting that horseracing – the sport of kings – took place here at Blickling. How long meets had been hosted here before the Earl's time is not known, but he promoted it by the construction of the Grandstand Tower in 1773, also by Thomas and William Ivory, affording fabulously far-reaching views. The side extension was added later when it was converted to a dwelling. It continues to be used as one to this day, as a unique holiday cottage.

Working the land

The 1729 survey of the estate commissioned by the 1st Earl shows much of the estate rented to tenant farmers, about 14 of them in all. The early features of the park, notably the avenues, cut across the landscape, apparently regardless of field boundaries, but agriculture was always of paramount concern at Blickling. As mentioned above, it was the agricultural income that supported the Hobarts' ambitions for the park's landscape and its many features.

Most of the farmhouses on the estate date from the 18th century, and they are mainly Grade II listed. As the estate grew, the Hobarts acquired both the land and the buildings used to farm it. Being amalgamated into one estate run by generations of the same family has resulted in these complexes surviving virtually intact. That agriculture was so vital to the continuation of Blickling has meant it has both formed and preserved the landscape you see today. Indeed, nine out of the 18 farmhouses are still lived in by farming families.

Below A view of the Grandstand Tower from Tower Park

Conserving Blickling

The 1st and 2nd Earls lavished attention on their family seat, each adding new treasures, but both making changes that respected its long history. The 2nd Earl's daughter was the last Hobart at Blickling but the family that followed took the same care to preserve their inheritance.

Caroline, Lady Suffield (d. 1850)

Caroline, Lady Suffield was the second daughter of the 2nd Earl. She inherited Blickling on her father's death, his sons having died in infancy and his eldest daughter having upset her father by divorcing the Earl of Belmore. Her sister Harriet remarried; another earl, but this one was destined to become a marquess, the 6th, of Lothian.

Caroline married William Assheton Harbord, who came into his title of Lord Suffield in 1810. The couple had no children and so when William died in 1821, Blickling passed to the Lothians, to Caroline's nephew, John Kerr, the 7th Marquess. However, Lady Suffield lived a long widowhood of over 30 years at Blickling. In that time she made her mark on Blickling, and made many improvements, particularly to the garden and park.

Lady Suffield outlived the 7th Marquess by nine years, so Blickling was inherited by his eldest son, William, the 8th Marquess of Lothian (see page 38) who could finally take full possession of the house and estate.

Top Caroline, Lady Suffield, who inherited Blickling in 1793; by Thomas Lawrence

Right William Assheton Harbord; after Karl Anton Hickel

Far right John William Robert Kerr, 7th Marquess of Lothian (1794–1841); after Sir Thomas Lawrence

In remembrance

Lady Suffield lived at Blickling for many years, and for 30 years after it had passed to her nephew. That was in 1821, and although from that year of her husband's death Blickling was no longer her property, it was during her widowhood that she began to make her mark here.

Caroline and her husband William had already commissioned one architectural project, that of a pyramidal mausoleum in memory of her father, the 2nd Earl, and his two wives. This was designed by Joseph Bonomi, modelled on the Roman pyramidal tomb of Cestius.

In the house Caroline did little more than introduce some Regency comforts. She did, however, recognise the importance of Richard Ellys' library in the Long Gallery and employed a librarian.

She had more influence on the park, and extended the boundaries of the estate to the River Bure when she bought a house, Blickling Lodge, and its land from a local solicitor, Mr Holly.

Continuing the vision

In the 1820s she turned her attention to the garden. From surviving designs and the respect she clearly had for her father, her extensive work here was a continuation of the vision the 2nd Earl had of informality and a recreated woodland effect. The man approached to incorporate her additions to the garden design was the son of Humphry Repton, last great English landscape designer of the 18th century.

John Adey Repton was more architect than landscape designer, but he worked with his father to produce architectural designs in the context of landscape gardening. Deaf from birth, he produced many sketches, which he must have used to communicate with his client, and for Lady Suffield he designed trellises, pedestals, alcove seats and a rustic temple adorned with fir cones. While he produced designs which survive, and indeed which have been used for recent additions to the garden (see opposite and page 59), the precise extent of his work remains unclear. It is thought he may also have been responsible for the linking arcades between the house and its service wings, and reconstructing the clock tower on the entrance front.

Above The Mausoleum designed by Joseph Bonomi, commissioned by Caroline in memory of her father, the 2nd Earl

Opposite left John Adey Repton's design for a trellis arbour, c.1825

Opposite right An arbour in the Dell Garden built along John Adey Repton's design

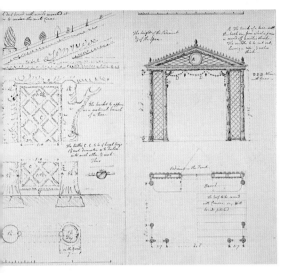

Generosity repaid

Lady Suffield supported the village school and had the cottages at the entrance to the park renovated. Many local people worked on the estate and Lady Suffield was a responsible employer and generous benefactor. In 1808 a fire might have destroyed the house if it hadn't been for the people of Aylsham who came to fight the blaze. Gifts of thanks were distributed in the town afterwards. A second fire broke out in April 1849 and further deeds of bravery were recorded by her land agent, Robert Parmeter: 'but for the courage of … the under Butler & principal Footman of Lady Suffield and Mr Wells the Innkeeper … who exposed themselves to the fire and smoke of the Room almost to suffocation until the Flames were extinguished … it would have been impossible to save the house'.

William, 8th Marquess of Lothian (1832–70) and Lady Constance Talbot (1836–1901)

Below left William, 8th Marquess of Lothian; by G. F. Watts

Below right Constance, Marchioness of Lothian; by John Leslie

When Blickling finally came into the possession of the Lothians, it became the property of William Kerr, 8th Marquess of Lothian, who was 18 at the time. He was educated at Oxford, where he met architect William Butterfield and decorative painter and architect John Hungerford Pollen, both of whom would make contributions at Blickling.

In 1854, at the age of 21, William married his first cousin, Constance Talbot. Although William's ancestral home was Newbattle Abbey in Roxburghshire, the couple decided to make Blickling their home. They spent the early years of their married life travelling, visiting France, Italy, India and Tibet. Before departing for Asia, William had a commemorative window to Lady Suffield installed at Blickling church, the joint effort of Butterfield and John Hardman, one of the pioneers of the stained-glass revival in the 19th century.

On their return in 1856, William and Constance began an energetic programme of improvements to the estate and early photographs of Blickling show the rooms furnished with items bought on their travels. One of the finest additions they made to Blickling's collection was a *cassonne* (pictured below). These large chests were one of the trophy furnishings of rich Italian merchants and aristocrats. A highly prized piece of furniture, it was traditionally given to a bride. A token of love from William to Constance perhaps?

Constance was a keen collector in her own right, her tastes shaped by her travels to far-flung places. A piece of Martinware (also pictured below) that Constance bought at a local craft fair may look as if it was fashioned in the Far East, but the Martin brothers were in fact based in Fulham. Martinware is highly ornate and often whimsical in design, and is important for the transition it marks from decorative Victorian ceramics to 20th-century studio pottery.

As well as changes inside the house, new terraces were made in the garden, the lake pushed back to its present position and the 18th-century woodland design revived. Constance and William poured their hearts and souls into their home and played an important part in Blickling's preservation.

Tragically, William died aged just 38 after a long illness. Finding herself a widow at 35, Constance continued to run the estate for many years and led a full and productive life. After Constance's death, as the couple had been childless, Blickling again passed to a nephew, Philip Kerr, 11th Marquess (see page 47).

William's improvements

Above The Long Gallery in the 19th century showing the original fireplace

William and Constance lived together at Blickling for 14 years, and as a newlywed couple started on an energetic programme of improvement at Blickling, making it both a more comfortable and fashionable house in which to live.

Their first job was to divide and enlarge the suite of rooms devised by the 2nd Earl (see page 27). A new morning room was created, naturally in this, the east front which would give them the best of the morning's sun, and by the end of 1857 it was 'in all the confusion and desolation of Bricklayers and carpenters'. William's architect for this work was Benjamin Woodward, who had worked on the Debating Hall at the Oxford Union, famously decorated by a team of young artists including Dante Gabriel Rossetti, William Morris and Edward Burne-Jones.

Another of William's acquaintances from Oxford, John Hungerford Pollen, was also involved in the decoration. At Blickling, Pollen created a fabulous beamed ceiling of intertwined birds and serpents in what is now the Brown Drawing Room. This ceiling was not to the taste of Philip Kerr, the 11th Marquess, and was hidden behind a suspended ceiling for many years, until a flood in 2002 revealed the extraordinary decoration.

Gothic imagery

Constance had her own sitting room at the north end of the east front, also with an elaborate ceiling designed by Pollen, but this has since been painted over. Where Pollen's work can be most seen and admired is in the Long Gallery.

Before work could begin, the entire Richard Ellys library had to be carefully removed. In 1859 the carpenters were able to get started, working to designs heavy with Gothic imagery and motifs from legend and nature. John O'Shea, a gifted sculptor who had worked with Woodward at the University Museum in Oxford, carved intricate and naturalistic foliage into uprights that were incorporated into the 1st Earl's bookcases. So elaborate were the designs that the carving is unfinished on one section near the south end.

The rest of the decoration was Pollen's, and the centrepiece of his design was a huge hooded stone chimneypiece, decorated with birds and bulls and a tree hung with heraldic shields. This was removed in the 1930s but a detailed drawing survives to show what a remarkable feature it would have been.

A large part of Pollen's decorative scheme, and one that survives, is the frieze full of figures from art and literature. Highly coloured and detailed, the frieze was key to the overall design but, like the carving, was left unfinished. This may be because William's vision exceeded his budget; the land agent

Robert Parmeter, who stayed on after Lady Suffield's death, wrote to his employer to express concern over the estate's finances.

Design for living

William made many other, more practical, modifications, introducing gas and installing a heating system in 1862. A major undertaking was the improvement of the layout of the domestic offices and servants' accommodation. The west wing was entirely rebuilt for this purpose, providing a new kitchen, laundry, brew-house (beer money was paid to servants in addition to a wage) and game larders. The Jacobean front wall was retained, however; for all his interest in modernising and improving, William was insistent that Blickling's appearance should not be changed or compromised.

Sadly, while these improvements were designed to make living more comfortable at Blickling, William did not enjoy them for long. He died in 1870, aged only 38.

Above left J. H. Pollen's chimneypiece design

Below The west wing of Blickling which William had rebuilt to house new domestic offices while preserving its Jacobean façade

A long widowhood

Above Constance, Lady Lothian in her widowhood

Right The elaborate parterre laid out in 1872

Opposite A detail of the 18th-century stone fountain at the centre of the Parterre

Constance stayed on at Blickling for another 30 years. As occupants of Blickling had done before her, she honoured the departed. As a memorial to her husband she commissioned an enormous alabaster statue of William, attended by life-size angels, to go in Blickling church. The rest of her long widowhood was devoted to the gardens.

In the 1820s Lady Suffield's changes to the garden had followed the informal, naturalistic scheme favoured by her father. By the mid-19th century the preference was for a more formal approach. At the same time the parterre was back in fashion. William had begun plans for such a parterre with the help of Sir Matthew Digby Wyatt and Markham Nesfield, but did not live long enough to see them carried out.

In 1872, two years after her husband's death and perhaps in his memory, Constance oversaw the creation of an elaborate sunken garden where there had once been a grand sweep of lawn from the woodland area to the east front. This required extensive excavation and the construction of a wall to contain it, with flights of steps and bays for seats. It was a complex and somewhat fussy arrangement of flowerbeds – over 80 in all – and topiary, all radiating out from an 18th-century fountain bought by the 1st Earl, which was placed in the centre in 1873.

The complicated design was entirely of Lady Lothian's devising, and she seems to have worked closely with her gardening staff. Such a feature would not have been possible without considerable manpower, and under head gardener Septimus Lyon was a staff of 15 gardeners. It was reported in a gardening journal in 1903, two years after Constance's death, that she 'had such a tender heart for the gardeners who had grown old in her service that, instead of pensioning them off, she kept them about the place to do light work'.

Bequeathing Blickling

The first half of the 20th century was a time of huge upheaval and change. Two world wars later and the country was a very different place. The large estates that had relied on local manpower had to adapt to this new social order, and Blickling led the way to a solution.

Below **Blickling** photographed from the air in 1931

A visionary thinker

After centuries of continuous occupation, from Lady Lothian's death in 1901 and for 30 years afterwards, Blickling was tenanted. The nephew of William and Constance, Philip Kerr, 11th Marquess of Lothian, inherited his title in 1930 and decided to make Blickling his principal English seat, although he only stayed here for short periods.

He reluctantly took up his role as landed gentry, having pursued a successful political career as a committed Liberal, with views founded on ideas of liberty and equality. He had been private secretary to Prime Minister Lloyd George, and was responsible for drafting the preface to the Treaty of Versailles, which ended the state of war between Germany and the Allied Powers in June 1919.

Having been at the centre of so much critical political activity, and given his political beliefs, it's hardly surprising that Lord Lothian didn't content himself with the quiet life of a country gentleman, of shooting parties, hunting meets and society balls. His other interests were travel and journalism, which he indulged after the First World War. He remained in politics and was for a while the Under-Secretary of State for India. However, he resigned this role as he found the administration's position on Free Trade incompatible with his own.

Lord Lothian was an idealist, a visionary thinker and writer, but he was also a man who got things done. Other than his involvement in a key event during the Second World War (see over), his most notable legacy, and one that changed the face of this country, was the Country Houses Scheme. Lord Lothian was instrumental in getting the National Trust Act through parliament in 1937, which enabled the first large-scale transfer of country houses to the National Trust in lieu of death duties. He consolidated this by his gift of Blickling to the nation.

But his gift was not an unwanted white elephant of a property. He invested much time and money in its repair and conservation before he handed it over to the National Trust.

When Lord Lothian died, the house, its contents and 2,025-hectare (5,000-acre) estate went to the National Trust. This extraordinarily generous and unprecedented bequest enabled the preservation of Blickling and paved the way for the subsequent acquisition by the National Trust of many of its major houses.

Left Philip Kerr, who served the nation's interests both during and after his lifetime

Philip Kerr,
11th Marquess of Lothian
(1882–1940)

Philip Kerr might not have expected to inherit Blickling, but the title and family home passed to him when his cousin Robert, 10th Marquess, died in 1930 with no offspring, as had several previous owners of Blickling.

Philip was something of an idealist, a man of vision and some might say an eccentric. Apparently his friends despaired of his untidy appearance, somewhat at odds with his importance as a politician. He had a profound influence not only on Blickling but also on world events at a crucial point in 20th-century history. In a letter to Roosevelt, Churchill referred to Philip as 'our Greatest Ambassador' because of the crucial part he played in bringing America into the Second World War. During his time as Ambassador to the USA (1939–40), Lord Lothian played a major role in encouraging the USA, then neutral, to supply Great Britain with weapons, warships and food to support our war effort, an act which arguably changed the course of history.

Lord Lothian's other legacy was two-fold: his inspiration in helping the National Trust to initiate the Country Houses Scheme, which has been fundamental to its success today; and a gift on a huge scale – Blickling.

Blickling Hall is an architectural masterpiece and, although Lord Lothian stayed here only for short periods, he made major changes while keeping true to the spirit of place, simultaneously creating a home and safeguarding a complete Norfolk estate.

'I venture to think that the country houses of Britain with their gardens, their parks, their pictures, their furniture and their peculiar architectural charm, represent a treasure of quiet beauty…'

'Next year [1941] is going to be a long, hard year. The war isn't won yet, but during that year we shall be grateful for and welcome any help that you can send us. It's going to make a great deal of difference.'

The Marquess makes good

Lord Lothian was clearly a driven and energetic individual. Not only did he hold positions in high office, not only was he founding editor of *The Round Table*, an influential journal devoted to Imperial and Commonwealth politics, but he also made many improvements to Blickling.

The house had been let to tenants from the time of Constance's death in 1901 until 1932. In that time the décor had not been kept in good repair and Lord Lothian found the house gloomy and drab.

He employed 33 workmen to bring Blickling up to date and it took them 14 months, painting over the high Victorian decoration or concealing it behind suspended ceilings. Lord Lothian bought Sheraton and Chippendale pieces to replace the dated Victorian furniture. He was apparently influenced by an article by Christopher Hussey that appeared in *Country Life* in 1930, which criticised the John Hungerford Pollen fireplace in the Long Gallery and Lady Lothian's Parterre; the latter was despairingly described by Hussey as a 'multiplicity of dotted beds'. The fireplace was destroyed – in hindsight a regrettable decision – but his choice of garden designer to simplify and improve the Parterre was an inspired one (see over).

The estate of the nation

Lord Lothian's improvements included the reorganisation of the servants' areas, in order to make the house function more efficiently. He had the kitchen remodelled and introduced some modern conveniences (see page 52).

The kitchen needed to function well, as on the occasions Lord Lothian did stay at Blickling, he hosted some important guests. Queen Mary came for lunch in 1938 (see page 53) and meetings of *The Round Table* would convene in the South Drawing Room, attended by domestic politicians and foreign diplomats. A staff of 12 domestic servants was required to keep house and garden in good order and, in the colder months, tend 36 fires. Lord Lothian's ownership of Blickling would be the last time the house was operated on a full scale; the consequences of the Second World War would lead to such a shift in the social order that many country houses and estates simply couldn't carry on as they had.

As well as rescuing Blickling from neglect and decay, Lord Lothian set in motion the events that would ensure its preservation in the future. The help he gave to the National Trust in setting up the Country Houses Scheme and his subsequent gift of the entire Blickling estate to the Trust make him one of the most influential British politicians you've never heard of. Philip Kerr died in Washington in December 1940.

Top Lord Lothian with Queen Mary in front of Blickling

Above Lord Lothian with Lord and Lady Astor

Above Lord Lothian welcoming guests in August 1934

The Marquess in the garden

By the time Norah Lindsay came to Blickling, she had already built up quite a reputation as a garden designer. Her own garden at Sutton Courtenay (see opposite) had been featured in *Country Life*, and her innovative work with Lawrence Johnston at Hidcote (also National Trust) had drawn considerable interest.

A gardener's palette

At Blickling she focused on the Parterre and the Temple Walk. The 'multiplicity of dotted beds' was replaced by four large squares. The 80 beds were reduced to 20. A disciple of Gertrude Jekyll, Norah was especially attentive to colour, using it as a painter uses a palette. In Blickling's Parterre she used a graduation of colours, from pink, blue, mauve and white near the house, but a concentration of yellow and orange to the east. Where Lady Lothian's colour scheme was uniformly riotous, Norah filled whole borders with cool colours to form backdrops to brighter hues. Her planting was always carefully considered, with regard to the overall effect as well as the seasons, designing borders to hit their high notes at different times of year.

On the Temple Walk her regard for how the area was experienced led to her decision to remove the avenue of yews that effectively marched the visitor to the Temple. Her planting of azaleas in subtly changing colours as the visitor progressed, merging into the trees around the Temple, was a brilliant and sensitive piece of design.

Other areas that Norah had a hand in designing were the plantings in the Moat, where she introduced hostas, buddleia, rosemary and hydrangeas.

Above **The Parterre**

Below The culmination of the Temple Walk with a salmon pink azalea in the foreground

The Marquess was a busy man seldom at Blickling and was not especially interested in running a large staff in the garden. The Parterre, Lady Lothian's complicated creation, was particularly in need of some simplification.

Two years before Lord Lothian moved to Blickling a less-than-complimentary account of the Parterre appeared in *Country Life*: 'To the modern eye the pattern area is too small in scale. The lines of the design are lost in a multiplicity of dotted beds, beautifully filled but without a perceptible reaction to each other or to the house.' The somewhat fussy Victorian design was firmly out of fashion, but fortunately the Marquess knew to whom to turn.

Norah Lindsay (1873–1948)

Above Norah Lindsay;
by G. F. Watts

Norah to remodel the gardens. She would 'live in' for the duration of her projects and indeed she spent most of her time moving from one country house to another, reportedly delighting her clients with her warmth and humour as well as her planting schemes.

'Her wit was extravagant, her conversation an ecstasy, her garden the finest in England, her appearance exotic to a degree.'
From the diary of Chips Channon

Hallmarks of Norah's style included the display of roses and herbaceous plants in separate beds. She would also group plants according to their colour, but she would enliven the layout by constantly varying the heights of plants and their leaf texture, to ensure there was plenty of interest for the viewer and the details of each plant were brought out in contrast with its neighbour. Again to keep her schemes varied and dynamic, she would place plants that flowered in spring next to those that flowered in summer next to those that flowered in autumn, for a continuous succession of blooms.

When Norah died in 1948 at the age of 75, she had become one of the most influential landscape gardeners of her time and indeed she is considered to be one of the greatest of the 20th century. Given the extent of her work and the acclaim it received it is surprising that only fragments of her garden designs remain. At Blickling we are fortunate to have a preserved example of her work in the form of the Parterre.

Norah Lindsay (née Bourke) was born in India into an Anglo-Irish upper-class military family. At the age of 22 she married Sir Harry Lindsay and went to live at her wedding gift, Sutton Courtenay Manor in Oxfordshire. Here, influenced by Gertrude Jekyll, she developed her skills as a gardener. Finding herself rather good at it and also in some financial difficulty following her divorce in 1924, she embarked on a career as a garden designer. Of course the wealthy circles in which she moved meant there was no shortage of large-scale commissions.

Shortly after inheriting the estate in 1930, and following the disparaging comments featured in Country Life, Lord Lothian engaged

An oral archive

A house, garden and estate as large as Blickling could not operate without a large staff, mostly local, some of whom had had generations of their family before them serve the household. At Blickling we are fortunate to have some of their experiences of working here on record.

The cook

Florence Copeland worked under the housekeeper, Miss O'Sullivan, as cook in the 1930s. Lord Lothian was only an occasional visitor to Blickling but when he inherited in 1930 he had the kitchen completely remodelled and re-equipped. From the early 1600s estates such as Blickling had ice houses – bunker-like brick-lined structures where the winter's ice would be stored and made use of through the year. Blickling still has its ice house, in a shady, woodland spot in the park, but Flo and her kitchen staff were fortunate to have a refrigerator, still a novelty item in the 1930s. She could even make her own ice cream, but she suspected Lord Lothian's main motive for getting the fridge was to chill the freshly squeezed orange juice to which he was particularly partial. However her range oven was tricky to use, having no thermometer: 'I put a sheet of paper in to test the temperature: if it turned light brown it was right for pies; if dark brown, it was hot enough for pastry.'

Her days were long, rising at 5am and retiring to bed at 10pm, but she remembered her days of service fondly. She catered for some notable visitors, including Prime Minister Stanley Baldwin and his wife in 1936, and even prepared a meal for royalty. Queen Mary came for an event called the Masque of Anne Boleyn in 1938, at which they ate eggs in aspic, quenelles of chicken with red pimentos and black truffles and a vanilla ice cream bombe.

The domestic service department of a country house was known as 'below stairs' and it was a literal description. Flo recalled that in all the years she worked at Blickling she was only permitted upstairs on three occasions, one being to see the dining room laid out for the royal luncheon party.

Left Flo the cook

Right Percy the gardener

Below The greenhouses in the Walled Garden in the 1930s

chrysanthemums…Well, you mention it, we grew it!' When Queen Mary came for the masque, the table was decorated with patriotic red, white and blue flowers.

The footman

John Payne came to work at Blickling as a footman in 1935 when he was 21 years old. A footman was originally a servant who would run beside or behind the carriages of aristocrats, to make sure they weren't overturned by obstacles such as ditches or tree roots. Footmen were something of a luxury and status symbol, and part of only the grandest households.

As Lord Lothian owned motor cars – to his friends' dismay he arrived at Westminster Abbey for the coronation of George VI in an Austin 7, the first affordable mass-produced vehicle – his footman became his chauffeur and John was promoted to this position, earning a pound a week plus tips.

The gardener

Percy Algate worked for Lord Lothian in Blickling's gardens under head gardener Mr Willey from 1934 to 1940. As well as vegetables from the Walled Garden for the table, the gardeners could grow soft fruit in the heated greenhouses and they also tended the formal areas, gathering in cut flowers for the house. Percy recalled: 'We had some lovely grape vines, peach houses, cucumbers, tomatoes,

The RAF at Oulton

Royal Air Force Oulton was a bomber base that was created on the Blickling estate in 1939 and was vital to the war effort before being closed for operations in 1946 and finally decommissioned in 1949. Over 3,000 RAF servicemen and women were billeted here within the grounds in Nissen huts, whilst RAF officers were housed in Blickling Hall.

The base was first home to 2 Group – the first group of squadrons to attack continental Europe. At this time the runways were grass, which were later replaced with concrete runways more suitable for use by heavy bombers. The base extended over a considerable area and remains of the airfield can still be seen in Oulton Street, just over a mile from the house. In 1944 the base became the centre for 100 Group, which flew covert radio and radar counter-measure missions. Flying operations ceased at the end of July 1945, after which Oulton was taken over by RAF Maintenance Command, which used the base to store de Havilland Mosquitos until November 1947.

This being the site where so many men and women served their country at a critical point in its history, many veterans' families treat RAF Oulton as a place of pilgrimage. Since 1995, the RAF Oulton Museum has been gathering and displaying objects, documents and oral histories relating to the working life of RAF Oulton, mostly from crew members of 100 Group as few who flew for 2 Group returned. The museum occupies the same space that was used as an officers' mess. Tell-tale

Top A Liberator crew in 1944

Left An aerial photograph of RAF Oulton taken in April 1944

remnants of graffiti as well as official records have confirmed this.

Whilst on operations, crews would spend time before and after each flight in a room designed to lower stress and improve morale. It also became an informal office for men writing letters and doing minor chores. The RAF Oulton Museum features a mock-up of a crew room, apparently a convincing one as an ex-crew member from RAF Oulton gave it his seal of approval, saying it brought back many memories.

The estate in wartime

The country house played a huge part in both world wars and many were transformed into training camps, hospitals and accommodation for land girls to help the war effort. As more and more men joined up, many never to return, the impact on the daily running of country estates grew ever greater, and the role of those left behind more significant.

One of the contributions made by the estate to the war effort was the supply of timber needed for pit props. During the First World War the overseas supply of timber had been disrupted and the mining industry had to go into overdrive to support manufacturing. So whole swathes of parkland were planted up with straight and fast-growing conifers. An area of the Blickling estate known as Hyde Park remained a conifer plantation until 1992.

The other large and lasting impact of wartime on the landscape was the 'Dig for Victory' campaign, which needed huge areas to go under cultivation to help feed the nation.

Most of the park was either ploughed or divided into fields for grazing cattle. Following the war, it took time for overseas trade to re-establish, with rationing continuing well into the 1950s. It was not until the 1970s that any significant restoration was begun at Blickling, and the areas first returned to grass were those around the lake which were most visible from the house.

Historic events

As already mentioned, Blickling had been involved in some key historical events but those of the 20th century arguably marked the greatest turning point in its long history. Without these events, Blickling would have remained private, away from public view. But not only Blickling – the Marquess's gift made possible the many great houses and beautiful gardens and spectacular landscapes in the care of the National Trust. It is difficult to overstate what Blickling represents and the impact it has had on our landscape and our accessibility to it.

Presenting Blickling

Blickling continues to play an important part in many people's lives. As an extensive and little-altered country estate, it provides homes and employment for farming families, some of whom have been here for 300 years and whose current members still work at Blickling today.

Left Visitors partaking in views of the Parterre

Vision and ambition

At the heart of Blickling is the mansion that proudly bears the Hobart arms. The house was designed to proclaim the status of its owners, but their vision and ambition stretched almost as far the eye can see. After all, the creation of a fine house is one thing, the ability to influence and form an entire landscape is something else.

Over the course of a year over 150,000 visitors come to Blickling, expecting to see a beautiful house – Grade I listed – furnished with fine things, and a well-tended garden – Grade II. This they will surely find, but it is the completeness of the estate that sets Blickling apart. Today, the estate of 2,025 hectares (5,000 acres) consists of lightly wooded, gently rolling arable land and includes the fields, woodlands, villages and farms that for centuries supported the lifestyle of Blickling's owners while providing a home and livelihood for the communities that lived here.

The other singular thing about Blickling is what it represents, to the people who work and volunteer here, to visitors and to an entire nation. That Blickling was a gift, the first of its kind, arising from one man's ideas about social and cultural access, makes it extraordinary and unique.

Top Staff replacing grilles in the Long Gallery; Blickling's library, itself a gift, is the largest in the Trust's care

Above Visitors watching actors perform in period costume

Keeping the garden trim and true

From the 17th to the early 20th century, two families developed the garden at Blickling, for the most part sensitively enhancing what went before. The yew hedges flanking the entrance, at around 400 years old, symbolise this history. Cutting these takes two people a fortnight each year but they are just a small part of what the National Trust has to do, and has plans to do, at Blickling.

Another iconic feature of the gardens at Blickling is the Parterre. This is one of the best surviving examples of Norah Lindsay's work. It may date from the 1930s but the work is not over. Now the National Trust has the responsibility of maintaining and developing it as she would have done and here, on the Parterre, in a nod to Blickling's latest incumbents, 16 yews have been cut to resemble acorns, taken from the National Trust's logo.

Continuing the tradition of sympathetic change and evolution, in 2005 the gardening team created the double borders to the south of the Parterre. Whilst these were a new feature, the team used the same techniques Norah Lindsay used to such effect in her remodelling of the Parterre in the 1930s. Just as she took great care over the arrangement of plants according to height, texture and colour, these 200-foot-long borders start with a grouping of cool colours – blue, mauve, pale pink and white – at the house end. The central section sees things warm up with yellows, oranges and browns before progressing into the hot borders, set alight with fiery scarlet and purple.

More recently, in 2009, a north-facing White Border was added, again bringing something new but paying tribute to Norah Lindsay's work. Also new to Blickling are the silverberries (or elaeagnus) at either end of the White Border, part of a national collection homed here in 2009.

Left Trimming yew on the Parterre into acorns, a nod to the people who care for the garden today

Renovation and renewal

North of the Parterre, the Wilderness hides a Secret Garden also recently renovated. While concerned with renewal, these plans simultaneously looked to the past and made use of the designs of John Adey Repton produced in the 1820s for Lady Suffield for a summerhouse and a wooden seat with trellis.

Also, 19th-century plant lists survive and continue to be used by the National Trust's gardening team. Where staff ran into double figures in the 1870s, when Constance created the first Parterre, there are now five gardeners under a head gardener. However, the gardening team is crucially supported by numerous volunteers, helping to develop and maintain one of the finest gardens in Norfolk.

Above The path to the Secret Garden

Below The double borders created in tribute to Norah Lindsay's work at Blickling

Pleasing and productive

These developments can be seen all over the garden. Close by the Wilderness is the 18th-century Orangery, recently furnished with 30 barrels of citrus plants, as it would have been in 1793. Next to this an area of woodland has been cleared to make way for an entirely new garden. Opened in 2010, the Orangery Garden has been stocked with a wide range of woodland plants, including camellia and varieties of mahonia. The woodland feel continues in the Dell Garden, which features spring colour with the early flowering of hellebore and foxglove. Over 100,000 bulbs have been planted here since 2005.

Elsewhere, the walled kitchen garden, so vital during and just after the Second World War, had sadly gone to seed, uncultivated and uncared for. Opened to the public in 2010, the visitor will now find it very much under the spade and, in season, serving up fresh produce for the restaurant; the garden providing for the house and its visitors, just as originally intended.

A view into the past

The Blickling estate is extensive and provides us with a valuable landscape, fast diminishing elsewhere. The estate has 200 hectares (500 acres) of woodland, an invaluable habitat to a great many species, both plant and animal, and all the more so given Norfolk is one of the least wooded counties in England.

The trees on the estate include some spectacular specimens, some veteran and some more recently planted to ensure the pattern of renewal at Blickling. In the garden behind the mansion, the Turkey oak (*Quercus cerris*), so-called as it is native to south-eastern Europe and Asia Minor, is still relatively young. Broader than it is tall, it measures over 27m (88ft) and could grow to 40m (130ft) in height. Oriental plane trees are found fringing the lawned Acre on the western side of the garden. In the summer months these provide shade if the visitor prefers relaxation to a game of croquet. Sequoia trees, too, cast quite a shadow; vigorous growers, they can reach a height of 10m (30ft) after 10 years, and 30–40m (100–130ft) after 50 years.

Cycle of change

In 1991 the Blickling estate was designated a Rural Conservation Area, the first in Norfolk, recognising the importance of the landscape and the many species it supports. The park may look much as it did in the 2nd Earl's day, but this is achieved not by leaving nature to its own devices, but rather by careful management by the Ranger team, which looks after the park, lake and the rest of the estate.

The Wilderness, planted during the 1680s after a great storm, was largely untouched since that time, although quite overgrown by the time the National Trust came to Blickling. It took another cataclysmic climatic event – the hurricane of 1987 that irrevocably damaged thousands of trees as well as the career of one television forecaster – for the latest cycle of change that continues to this day.

Above The Kitchen Garden oak and Davy, Lord Lothian's head woodman

Below Plane trees are known for their longevity and spreading crowns

Managing the land

The park includes swathes of grassy pasture as well as wooded and watery habitats that are little changed since the 1830s. The human inhabitants of Blickling may have had a more obvious influence over the landscape, but the abundant wildlife found here is a key feature of the estate and one that requires as careful management as the rest.

Much of the estate is used for farming and that activity, millennia old, has had a profound effect on wildlife. When the first farmers cleared woodland for the plough, animals such as skylarks, grey partridges and brown hares increased. Much, much later, when agriculture became intensified in the second half of the 20th century, many species were again affected, with some, such as the corn bunting, tree sparrow and stone curlew, declining close to the point of disappearance on arable land, and others, such as the red-backed shrike and great bustard, disappearing altogether.

Likewise, hedges traditionally used as field margins were made of hawthorn, blackthorn, field maple and elm. They provided nesting sites for such birds as whitethroats, yellowhammers and partridges. Again, with the intensification of agriculture, thousands of miles of hedges were destroyed to create larger, more productive fields in which large machinery could operate. As a result, huge areas of hedgerow habitat, and the rough grass which grows around its roots, were lost.

Above The lake is an important habitat managed with care for the species that live and hunt here

Right Farming today

Modern farming methods

While the term wildlife suggests something separate from human activity, at Blickling and throughout the UK it is our use of the land that determines the success and survival of many species. So while Blickling remains a farmed landscape and supports many families in this activity, farming is now practised with much more sensitivity to the environment. There is widespread grazing with low chemical input on the grassland in the Bure Valley, and sustainable but commercial arable farming is practised on the flatter, drier ground.

New management

Under the management of the National Trust and with the help of Blickling's tenant farmers work is ongoing to restore lost habitats. Such work includes the management of grass strips at the edges of fields for barn owls to hunt and skylarks to forage in. Indeed barn owls thrive at Blickling, nesting in the many old trees and farm buildings. Restoration work at the lake has brought reed buntings, sedge warblers and reed warblers to the waterside vegetation. On the lake you'll also see mallards, grebes and a variety of geese.

Other important winged species include the colonies of bats found here. At Blickling there are various species: Daubenton's, a medium-sized bat species, sometimes known as the water bat or hairy-footed bat; Natterer's, one of the mouse-eared bat species, named after an Australian naturalist rather than any noise it emits; the common Pipistrelle, tiny bats with reddish-brown coats; Noctule, one of the largest British species and usually the first bat to appear in the evening; and the Brown Long-Eared, with ears almost as long as its body. Bats of any kind are a vital part of our native wildlife and they can tell us a lot about the wildlife not seen, such as the insects they feed on. They are particularly sensitive to changes in land-use practices.

Above Generations of farming families have worked the land here at Blickling; this family group lived at Heath Farm

A complete picture

The Blickling estate boasts a mansion, nine farms, over 120 cottages and houses, many of which are still called home, over 1,850 hectares (around 4,600 acres) of land and one of the finest gardens in Norfolk. However, it is fair to say that Blickling is much more than the sum of its parts.

This page Early morning on the Blickling Hall estate

There is so much to Blickling, it would be difficult to see and experience it all in a day. Indeed there is much more that could be written about Blickling, not least because the story doesn't end here.

When the 11th Marquess presented Blickling to the National Trust it was a single act of extraordinary generosity, but it was also an instruction to carry on the work to keep the country's great houses and gardens open and accessible to the public.

At the time of writing, 75 years after Lord Lothian's death, the National Trust looks after historic houses, gardens, mills, coastline, forests, farmland, moorland, islands, castles, nature reserves, villages … the list goes on. The work to keep these places special also goes on and the National Trust continues to find imaginative ways of adding new layers while revealing the past. At Blickling the Hobarts not only looked back to Sir Henry's grand plan but also into the future and beyond their estate boundaries as they developed that ambition. Similarly, the National Trust uses its knowledge of Blickling's past to help ensure its future.